Heinemann First
ENCYCLOPEDIA

Volume 10
Rus-Spi

Heinemann Library
Chicago, Illinois

© 1999, 2006 Heinemann Library
a division of Reed Elsevier Inc.
Chicago, Illinois

Customer Service   888–454–2279

Visit our website at www.heinemannlibrary.com

Series Editors: Rebecca and Stephen Vickers, Gianna Williams
Author Team: Rob Alcraft, Catherine Chambers, Sabrina Crewe, Jim Drake, Fred Martin, Angela Royston, Jane Shuter, Roger Thomas, Rebecca Vickers, Stephen Vickers

This revised and expanded edition produced for Heinemann Library by Discovery Books.
Photo research by Katherine Smith and Rachel Tisdale
Designed by Keith Williams, Michelle Lisseter, and Gecko
Illustrations by Stefan Chabluk and Mark Bergin

Originated by Ambassador Litho Limited
Printed in China by WKT Company Limited

10 09 08 07 06
10 9 8 7 6 5 4 3 2

Library of Congress Cataloging-in-Publication Data

Heinemann first encyclopedia.
     p.   cm.
    Summary: A fourteen-volume encyclopedia covering animals, plants, countries, transportation, science, ancient civilizations, US states, US presidents, and world history
    ISBN 1-4034-7117-7 (v. 10 : lib. bdg.)
    1. Children's encyclopedias and dictionaries.
I. Heinemann Library (Firm)
AG5.H45 2005
031—dc22   2005006176

Acknowledgments
Cover: Cover photographs of a desert, an electric guitar, a speedboat, an iceberg, a man on a camel, cactus flowers, and the Colosseum at night reproduced with permission of Corbis. Cover photograph of the Taj Mahal reproduced with permission of Digital Stock. Cover photograph of an x-ray of a man reproduced with permission of Digital Vision. Cover photographs of a giraffe, the Leaning Tower of Pisa, the Statue of Liberty, a white owl, a cactus, a butterfly, a saxophone, an astronaut, cars at night, and a circuit board reproduced with permission of Getty Images/Photodisc. Cover photograph of Raglan Castle reproduced with permission of Peter Evans; J. Allan Cash Ltd., pp. 4, 7, 9, 22 bottom, 23, 25, 30, 31, 36 bottom, 44, 46 left, 47; British Museum, p. 10 right; Forest Life Picture Library, p. 10 left; The Hutchison Library, pp. 5, 24 bottom; L. Taylor, p. 24; Doug Allan, p. 17 top; Martyn Colbeck, p. 14 top; J.A.L. Cook, p. 8 bottom; Corbis, p. 29 bottom; Mary Deebie and Victoria Stone, p. 14 bottom; Melanie Friend, p. 20; Richard Hermann, p. 15 bottom; Hulton Archive/Getty Images, p. 26 bottom; Rudie Kuiter, p. 12; MPI/Getty Images, pp. 6 bottom, 26 top; Richard Ray, p. 28 top; L.L.T. Rhodes, p. 21 bottom; James Robinson, p. 16 right; Norbert Rosing, p. 17 bottom; Kjell Sandved, p. 15 top; Wendy Shattil and Bob Rozinski, p. 28 bottom; S. Solum/PhotoLink, pp. 42, 43; David Tipling, p. 16 left; Tom Ulrich, p. 22 top; P. and W. Ward, p. 8 top; Barrie Watts, p. 11 top; Doug Wechsler, p. 11 bottom; Robert Wu, p. 13 top; Science Photo Library, p. 27 bottom; Bruce Coleman Ltd., Gunter Ziesler, p. 35 bottom; Ingrid Hudson, p. 40; Trevor Page, p. 38; Oxford Scientific Films/Kathie Atkinson, p. 36 top; Neil Bromhall, p. 32 bottom; J.A.L. Cooke, pp. 34 bottom; Donald Specker, p. 32 top; Survival Anglia/Dr. F. Koster, p. 41; David Hardy, pp. 37, 45 top; Richard Megna, p.39 bottom; Hank Morgan, p. 39 top; NASA, p. 45 bottom, p. 46 right.

Welcome to
Heinemann First Encyclopedia

What is an encyclopedia?

An encyclopedia is an information book. It gives the most important facts about many different subjects. This encyclopedia has been written for children who are using an encyclopedia for the first time. It covers many of the subjects from school and others you may find interesting.

What is in this encyclopedia?

In this encyclopedia, each topic is called an *entry*. There is one page of information for every entry. The entries in this encyclopedia explain

- animals
- plants
- dinosaurs
- countries
- geography
- history
- world religions
- music
- art
- transportation
- science
- technology
- states
- famous Americans

How to use this encyclopedia

This encyclopedia has thirteen books called *volumes*. The first twelve volumes contain entries. The entries are all in alphabetical order. This means that Volume 1 starts with entries that begin with the letter A and Volume 12 ends with entries that begin with the letter Z. Volume 13 is the index volume. It also has other interesting information.

Here are two entries that show you what you can find on a page:

The "see also" line tells you where to find other related information.

This is the letter that the entry starts with.

Fact boxes give you details about the topic.

Did You Know? boxes have fun or interesting bits of information.

The Fact File tells you important facts and figures.

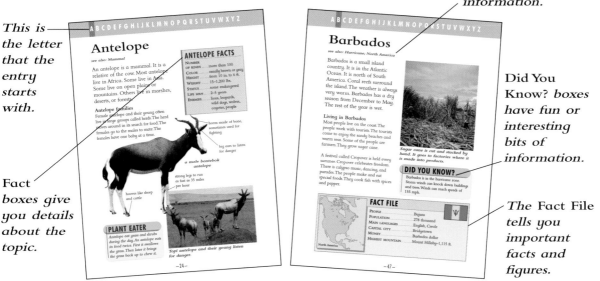

Russia

see also: Asia, Europe

Russia is a very large country. Part of it is in Europe. Part of it is in Asia. The Ural Mountains divide Europe from Asia. The north of Russia is inside the Arctic Circle. The south is dry and much warmer.

Living in Russia

Farmers in the west of Russia grow wheat, potatoes, and other crops. They also raise cattle. There is mining for coal and metals, and drilling for oil and gas. Factory workers make everything from matchsticks to microwaves. Most people in the cities live in apartment buildings. About one-fourth of Russians live in rural areas. Some Russians who live in the forests still live in traditional wooden huts called *izba*.

Many different groups of people live in Russia. Each group has its own customs, music, and dancing.

St. Basil's Cathedral is in Moscow's Red Square. It is famous for its onion-shaped roofs. A big May Day parade is held in Red Square each year.

DID YOU KNOW?

Russia and fourteen smaller countries were called the Soviet Union until 1991.

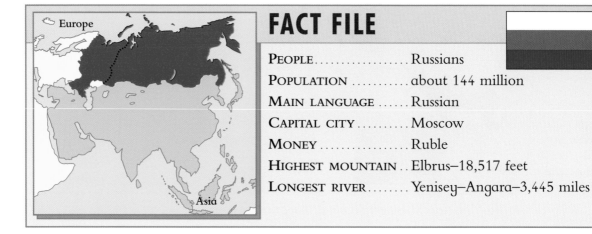

FACT FILE

PEOPLE	Russians
POPULATION	about 144 million
MAIN LANGUAGE	Russian
CAPITAL CITY	Moscow
MONEY	Ruble
HIGHEST MOUNTAIN	Elbrus—18,517 feet
LONGEST RIVER	Yenisey–Angara–3,445 miles

Rwanda

see also: Africa

Rwanda is a small country in the middle of Africa. There are mountains and forests. It is warm and wet all year round.

Living in Rwanda

Most families in Rwanda live in small houses that they build themselves. These houses have mud walls. The roofs are made from the leaves of banana trees. Most houses also have a small garden where the family grows its own food. They grow bananas, sweet potatoes, and a plant called cassava. The roots of the cassava plant are used to make flour. Some farmers grow coffee and tea to sell to other countries.

There are two main tribes, or groups, in Rwanda. They are called the Hutu and the Tutsi. Fights started in 1994 between the Hutu and the Tutsi. Many Rwandans were killed in the fighting.

Rwanda has some of the tallest and shortest people on Earth. The Tutsi dancers shown here are very tall. The Twa people, known as Pygmies, also live in Rwanda. They are some of the smallest people in the world.

DID YOU KNOW?

Mountain gorillas in Rwanda are an endangered species. Very few of these gorillas are left because of armies fighting and illegal hunters who kill gorillas.

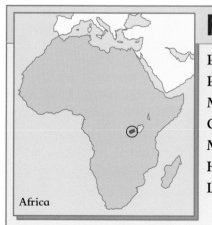

Africa

FACT FILE

PEOPLE	Rwandans
POPULATION	almost 8 million
MAIN LANGUAGES	Kinyarwanda and French
CAPITAL CITY	Kigali
MONEY	Rwandan franc
HIGHEST MOUNTAIN	Mount Karisimbi—14,792 feet
LONGEST RIVER	Kagera—248 miles

Sacagawea

see also: Lewis and Clark

Sacagawea was a guide and interpreter for the explorers Lewis and Clark. She was a Shoshone Indian. Her people lived in the northwest of North America.

Sacagawea and Charbonneau

Around 1800, Sacagawea was captured by Hidatsa warriors. She went to live in a Hidatsa village in what is now North Dakota. There, she became the wife of a French fur trader named Toussaint Charbonneau.

Traveling with Lewis and Clark

In 1804, the Lewis and Clark expedition from the United States arrived. Charbonneau said he and Sacagawea would go with the expedition as interpreters and guides. They set off in spring. Sacagawea had a new baby.

No one really knows what Sacagawea looked like.

Sacagawea leads Lewis and Clark to the Pacific Ocean.

DID YOU KNOW?

Another story says that Sacagawea did not die in 1812. It says she was living on a Shoshone Indian reservation in Wyoming until 1884.

Sacagawea was a useful guide. She found plants for food and medicine. She showed the men important trails. Sacagawea reassured other Indians that the expedition was peaceful and friendly. She helped trade for horses.

After the expedition returned, records say she gave birth to a daughter in 1812. She died of fever a few months later.

KEY DATES

1788–1790	Sacagawea is born.
ABOUT 1800 ..	Sacagawea is kidnapped.
1800–1803	Sacagawea marries Toussaint Charbonneau.
1804–1806	Lewis and Clark expedition.
1812 OR 1884 .	Sacagawea dies.

Saudi Arabia

see also: Asia, Islam

Saudi Arabia is a country in the Middle East. Most of Saudi Arabia is a hot desert. It has sand dunes, stones, and bare rock. Snakes, lizards, rats, and wild cats live in the desert. There are mountains in the west.

Living in Saudi Arabia

About half of the people work in farming. Farmers grow wheat, bananas, and dates in areas where there is water. Some Saudis have herds of goats and camels. There is oil in the rocks under Saudi Arabia. The oil is sold to other countries.

Almost everyone in Saudi Arabia is a follower of the religion of Islam. The holy city of Islam is Mecca in Saudi Arabia. Followers of Islam try to make a special journey to Mecca once in their lives. This journey is called a pilgrimage.

At this market in Saudi Arabia all goods of one type are sold together. Here leather goods are on sale.

DID YOU KNOW?

The Saudi flag has Arabic writing on it. The Saudi flag is one of only a few national flags with words.

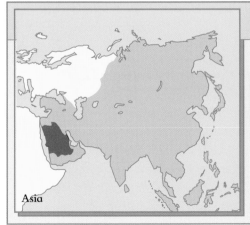

Asia

FACT FILE

PEOPLE	Saudis
POPULATION	about 25 million
MAIN LANGUAGE	Arabic
CAPITAL CITY	Riyadh
MONEY	Saudi riyal
HIGHEST MOUNTAIN	Jabal Sawda—10,283 feet

Scorpion

see also: Invertebrate

A scorpion is a small animal. It has two large claws on its front legs and it has six other legs. A scorpion has a curved tail. The tail has a sharp stinger on the end. Scorpions are hunters. They live mainly in warm parts of the world. The scorpion is from the same group of animals as the spider.

Scorpion families

Female scorpions have lots of babies. They look like tiny, see-through, adult scorpions. Scorpions hide under rocks or in holes in the daytime. They like cool, damp places out of the sun's heat.

SCORPION FACTS	
NUMBER OF KINDS	more than 1,400
COLOR	black or brown
LENGTH	half inch to 6 ½ inches
STATUS	rare
WEIGHT	from less than one ounce to over an ounce
ENEMIES	owls, frogs, snakes, rats

a thick-tailed scorpion

stinger to kill food and enemies

jointed tail with a deadly sting

strong claws for grabbing food

jaws for tearing food into small pieces

Babies ride on the mother's back for about a year. Then they look after themselves.

INSECT AND MEAT EATER

Scorpions hunt at night. They use their poisonous stings to kill insects, centipedes, spiders, and lizards. Scorpions can live in the driest places. They can go without water for months. They can live without food for more than a year.

Scotland

see also: Europe, United Kingdom

Scotland is one of the four main parts of the United Kingdom. Mountains cover much of Scotland. There are many long inlets and islands around the west coast.

Living in Scotland

The two biggest cities in Scotland are Glasgow and Edinburgh. Not many people live in the mountains or on the islands. Some Scots make a living by farming and fishing. Others look after the tourists in hotels.

Scottish people sometimes wear clothes made from a special patterned, woolen cloth. It is called tartan. Each family, or clan, has its own pattern and colors.

Every year the Scottish Highland games include a variety of sports. This sportsman wearing a tartan kilt is throwing the hammer.

DID YOU KNOW?

Loch Ness is a lake in the Scottish Highlands. It is famous for the sightings of a large animal called the Loch Ness Monster. Some people believe the animal is real. Other people do not think it exists at all.

Europe

FACT FILE

PEOPLE	Scots, Scottish
POPULATION	about 5 million
MAIN LANGUAGES	English and Scottish Gaelic
CAPITAL CITY	Edinburgh
BIGGEST CITY	Glasgow
MONEY	Pound sterling
HIGHEST MOUNTAIN	Ben Nevis—4,411 feet
LONGEST RIVER	Tay River—120 miles

Sculpture

see also: Art

Sculpture is works of art, such as statues and other objects. A sculpture can show a real object. It can also be an image that tries to show a feeling or an idea. A person who makes sculptures is called a sculptor.

Making sculptures

Sculpture can be made of almost any material. Very hard materials, such as stone or metal, are often used. Hard materials last a long time. Stone and wood are chipped and carved. Metal, plaster, and plastic sculptures are usually made by pouring liquid into a mold.

This huge wooden sculpture of a chair is on display in a forest. It is made from wood grown in the forest.

A sculpture of a human or animal figure is called a statue. Statues like this were sometimes used as columns on buildings in ancient Greece and Rome.

Sea Anemone

see also: Sea Life

A sea anemone is a sea animal with a soft body. It has no bones. Different sea anemones live in shallow seas and rockpools near the seashore. They are found all over the world. Sea anemones are members of the same group of animals as jellyfish and corals.

Sea anemone families

Some sea anemones lay eggs to make baby anemones. Other kinds make more anemones by dividing off parts of their own bodies. A sucker keeps the sea anemone stuck in the same place. This is where it will spend most of its life.

SEA ANEMONE FACTS

NUMBER OF KINDS	more than 9,000
COLOR	all colors
LENGTH	1 to 3 inches
STATUS	common
LIFE SPAN	up to hundreds of years
ENEMIES	sea slugs, fish

tentacles to feel for food

a beadlet anemone

big mouth so tentacles can easily push food into it

tentacles covered in thousands of little stings to kill food

This green sea anemone is eating a crab.

MEAT EATER

Sea anemones eat animals such as shrimp and small fish. They use the stingers on the tentacles around their mouths to catch and kill animals. The tentacles push the food into its open mouth.

Sea Horse

see also: Fish

A sea horse is a very strange fish. Its head looks like a horse's head. It has a curved tail and a long, sucking mouth. Sea horses live in warm seas all over the world.

Sea horse families

Female sea horses lay eggs in the male sea horse. He has a special pouch to hold the eggs. When the eggs hatch, the male sea horse opens the pouch. The babies swim out.

SEA HORSE FACTS

NUMBER OF KINDS	35
COLOR	changes to match surroundings
LENGTH	up to 12 inches
STATUS	common
ENEMIES	other fish, people

MEAT EATER

Sea horses are too slow to chase and to catch food. So they hold perfectly still. They wait for food to come to them. When small shrimp or little fish swim past, the sea horse sucks them up like a vacuum cleaner.

long mouth sucks up food

tough, bony body for protection

back fin pushes the sea horse through water

grasping tail to hold still while waiting for food

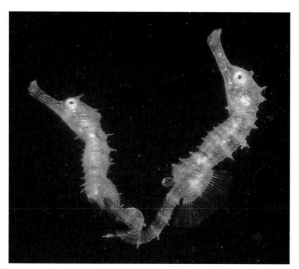

These newly hatched, short-snouted sea horses are able to swim away as soon as they are born.

a White's sea horse

Sea Life

see also: Coral, Fish

Most of the world is covered by the sea. Many plants and animals live or feed in the sea. Most sea life is near the top of the water. This is where there is plenty of light. Some creatures live in the deep sea where it is dark.

Some of the creatures that live deep in the sea look very strange. This hatchetfish lights up.

Living in the sea

Plants and animals need oxygen to live. Most sea animals take oxygen from the water. Sea plants use sunlight to make oxygen and food. Seabirds and mammals that live in the sea breathe the air at the surface of the water.

Most sea life is made of tiny creatures and plants called plankton. They live in the sunlight near the top of the sea. Many sea animals eat plankton. Even the largest whales eat plankton. Fish are in all the seas around the world.

Most fish stay near the surface, but some live on the bottom of the sea. Mollusks, such as shellfish and octopus, sit on the bottom of the sea. Crustaceans, such as crabs and shrimp, also live on the bottom. They eat bits of dead plants and animals that sink.

DID YOU KNOW?

Coral reefs are found in shallow, warm water. Many different creatures live on and around coral reefs. Corals reefs are made by millions of tiny coral polyps.

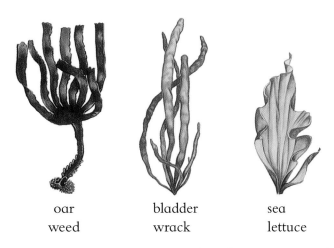

oar weed   bladder wrack   sea lettuce

There are 7,000 kinds of seaweed. They look very different in shape, size, and color. Seaweed can be used for food, fertilizer, and medicines.

Sea Lion

see also: Mammal, Sea Life

A sea lion is a mammal. It lives in the sea. It comes onto beaches to have its babies. Sea lions live in the Pacific and Atlantic Oceans. They can move faster than a person on land. They can swim as fast as 25 miles per hour.

Sea lion families

A male sea lion is called a bull. A female sea lion is called a cow. A baby sea lion is called a pup. A bull marks out a territory. It gets as many cows as possible to stay there. Each female has one pup at a time. She feeds the pup on milk for about six months. Then it is old enough to hunt for its own food.

SEA LION FACTS

NUMBER OF KINDS	5
COLOR	light brown
LENGTH	up to 7 feet
WEIGHT	up to 600 lbs.
STATUS	common
LIFE SPAN	up to 15 years
ENEMIES	killer whales, people

good eyes for seeing food

ears to listen underwater for food

long, smooth body to help push through the water

a South American sea lion

back flippers to swim straight or turn quickly in the water

strong front flippers for swimming fast

These Steller's sea lions are gathering on a beach to mate.

MEAT EATER

A sea lion eats fish, squid, and octopus. It can see very well. It chases its prey through the water.

Sea Urchin

see also: Sea Life

A sea urchin is a ball-shaped animal. It has a hard, spiny skin. Sea urchins live in seas all over the world. They are one of the very oldest kinds of sea creatures.

Sea urchin families

Sea urchins lay eggs. They send the eggs floating off into the sea. The eggs hatch into tiny sea urchins. Adult sea urchins do not take care of the eggs or the babies.

Sea urchins move around on hundreds of special tube feet. Each tube has suckers on it. Sea urchins use the suckers to grip onto underwater rocks.

SEA URCHIN FACTS

NUMBER OF KINDS	700
COLOR	all colors
SIZE	2 to 12 inches across
STATUS	common
LIFE SPAN	about 10 years
ENEMIES	fish, people

sharp spines protect against enemies; some sea urchins have poisonous spines

a sea urchin

spines that grow again if they are snapped off

These white sea urchins are eating a skin that was shed by a lobster.

PLANT AND MEAT EATER

A sea urchin uses the five moving pincers around its mouth to scrape up algae and small animals, such as coral.

Seabird

see also: Bird, Gull

A seabird is any kind of bird that feeds in the sea. Gulls and terns are seabirds. Some ducks, geese, and swans are seabirds, too. Some seabirds, like the albatross, spend much of their lives at sea. They only visit land to breed.

Seabird families

Different seabirds have different kinds of family life. All seabirds lay their eggs on land. Most seabirds have nests. Some nests are in trees or cliffs. Other nests are on the beach or in the grass. Some seabirds nest in burrows in the ground. Both male and female seabirds feed their chicks.

SEABIRD FACTS

COLOR	mostly white, gray, or black
LENGTH	10 inches to 4 feet
WEIGHT	2 ounces to 26 lbs.
STATUS	most are common
LIFE SPAN	5 to 30 years
ENEMIES	land animals that eat eggs and attack chicks

MEAT EATER

Most seabirds eat fish, squid, or shellfish. Some seabirds can dive deep into the sea. Other seabirds pick up food close to the surface.

The puffin has a large and colorful bill. The bill can hold many small fish at one time.

The cormorant dives from the sky into the water to catch fish. Then it dries its wings before it flies again.

Seal

see also: Mammal, Sea Lion

The seal is a mammal. It lives in the sea. There are many kinds of seals all over the world. Many seals live in cold water. Some live in warm water. Fur seals have thick fur. Most other seals have shiny, waterproof short hair.

Seal families

A male seal is called a bull. A female seal is called a cow. A baby seal is called a pup. Bulls are usually much bigger than cows. The bulls usually swim to land in the spring before the cows do. Each bull chooses a bit of land. Then he tries to get cows to move onto his land.

A cow has only one pup each year. Pups are born with special furry coats to keep them warm. Cows feed their pups on milk until the pups can hunt for fish and squid.

SEAL FACTS

NUMBER OF KINDS	19
COLOR	gray or brown
LENGTH	some kinds up to 16 feet
WEIGHT	some kinds up to 6,000 lbs.
STATUS	some are rare
LIFE SPAN	up to 38 years
ENEMIES	killer whales, people

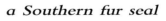

big eyes for seeing in murky water

waterproof fur and thick blubber to keep warm in cold water

flippers for swimming

a Southern fur seal

MEAT EATER

Most seals eat fish, shellfish, and squid. The leopard seal eats penguins. Seals can dive very deep under water to chase food.

These harp seal pups have white fur. It is hard to see them in the snow.

Season

see also: Climate, Weather

Seasons are the different times of the year. Each season has its own kind of weather. The seasons happen at about the same time every year.

The four seasons

Some places have four seasons: spring, summer, fall, and winter.

Spring The days get longer. Plants begin to grow. Many farmers sow their seeds. Some animals mate in the spring. Other animals give birth.

Summer It is warm. There is plenty of light. The days are long. Plants grow and make food for animals. Many animals raise their young.

Fall The days get shorter. Crops ripen and are harvested.

Winter It is colder. The days are short. The nights are long. Most plants stop growing. Some plants lose their leaves. There is less food for animals. Some animals hibernate. Other animals migrate to warmer places.

In the fall, the leaves of some types of trees change from green to bright red, orange, and yellow.

Some places that do not have four seasons have dry and rainy seasons. This shows a storm during the rainy season in Malaysia.

DID YOU KNOW?

Some places have no seasons at all. The days are always about the same length near the equator. This part of the world is hot and wet. Tropical rain forests are always hot and wet. Some deserts are always hot and dry.

Seed

see also: Crop, Plant

The seed is the part of a plant that may take root in the ground. It may grow into a new plant. Nuts and grains are seeds. Fruits have seeds inside them.

The life of a seed

A seed comes from a flower. The seeds inside the flower swell and ripen as the flower's petals wilt and die. Birds, animals, water, and wind help to scatter different kinds of seeds. A new plant may grow when a seed falls to the ground and starts to grow in the soil.

A seed stores food. People and animals eat the seeds of many plants. Nuts are seeds protected by hard shells. Grain is the seed of wheat. Grain is ground into flour to make bread and pasta. Rice, beans, peas, and sweetcorn are all seeds. They can be cooked and eaten.

Stage 1 The root pushes its way out of the seed into the soil.

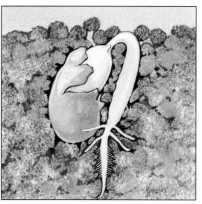

Stage 2 The root continues to grow. The stem begins to push its way out of the soil.

Stage 3 The stem grows above the soil. Leaves start to grow out of the seed.

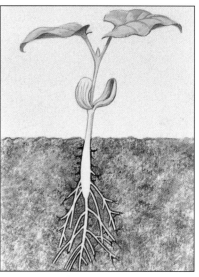

Stage 4 The root, stem, and leaves grow into a little plant.

Pendleton Community Library

These pictures show the four stages of the growth of a seed into a plant.

Serbia and Montenegro

see also: Europe

Serbia and Montenegro is a country in eastern Europe. There is lowland with rivers in the north. There are mountains and hills in the center and south. Summers are warm. Winters are cold. The coast is hot.

Living in Serbia and Montenegro

About half the people live in rural areas. Farmers grow grain, sugar beets, potatoes, cotton, and grapes. They raise pigs, sheep, and cattle. There is also mining. Factories make textiles and machinery.

Serbia and Montenegro used to be part of Yugoslavia. In 1992 Slovenia, Croatia, Macedonia, and Bosnia-Herzegovina became independent from Yugoslavia. In 2003 Yugoslavia divided into the two republics of Serbia and Montenegro.

Many people work in the shops and offices of the capital city of Belgrade.

DID YOU KNOW?

Serbian food mixes things together. One popular dish has fried peppers, bacon, prunes, tomatoes, and spices.

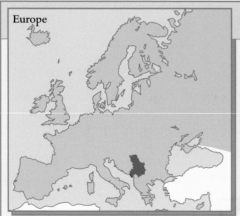

Europe

FACT FILE

PEOPLE	Serbians, Montenegrins
POPULATION	almost 11 million
MAIN LANGUAGE	Serbo-Croatian
CAPITAL CITY	Belgrade
MONEY	Serbian dinar, Euro
HIGHEST MOUNTAIN	Mount Daravica—8,714 feet
LONGEST RIVER	Danube River—1,777 miles

Shark

see also: Fish

A shark is a fish. Different kinds of sharks live in oceans and seas all over the world. Most sharks live in warm water. The great white shark, the blue shark, the tiger shark, and the leopard shark sometimes attack people.

Shark families

Little is known about shark families. The female shark gives birth to babies. They swim away on their own. Some kinds of sharks have as many as 80 babies at a time.

Young sharks are called pups. They stay close to the coasts. They only go into deep water after they have grown bigger.

SHARK FACTS

NUMBER OF KINDS	340
COLOR	white, yellow, gray, or blue
LENGTH	usually up to 20 feet (whale shark 66 feet long)
WEIGHT	usually up to 2,650 lbs. (whale shark 15,400 lbs.)
STATUS	great white shark is rare
LIFE SPAN	about 35 years
ENEMIES	big sharks that eat smaller sharks; people

high back fin to turn around quickly

long side fins move to keep the shark level and to keep it from sinking

long tail swishes to build up speed

a great white shark

sharp teeth to hold and cut food

MEAT EATER

A shark eats fish. It catches them with its sharp teeth. Some sharks can smell blood in the water. Big sharks, like the tiger shark, will eat turtles and seals. The whale shark is the world's biggest shark. It eats only tiny creatures called krill and plankton.

The great white shark has two rows of sharp teeth.

Sheep

see also: Mammal

A sheep is a mammal. It has a long, warm, woolly coat. It has special feet so it can live on mountains and hills. There are many different types of sheep. Farmers around the world keep sheep. Sheep are raised for their meat, milk, and wool.

Sheep families

A male sheep is called a ram. A female sheep is called a ewe. A baby sheep is called a lamb. A ewe has one or two lambs each year. Ewes, lambs, and one or two rams live in a large group called a flock. The female lambs stay in the flock after they have grown up. Most male lambs raised by farmers are sold for meat.

SHEEP FACTS

NUMBER OF KINDS	914
COLOR	usually white or brown
HEIGHT	up to 5 feet
LENGTH	up to 5 feet
WEIGHT	up to 300 lbs.
STATUS	common
LIFE SPAN	up to 20 years
ENEMIES	wolves, eagles, crows

some rams have horns for fighting

wool coat to keep warm

soft, split hooves for good balance when walking on rocks and hard ground

a sheep

PLANT EATER

A sheep eats grass and the leaves of small bushes. Some sheep have very tough mouths. This helps them to eat prickly leaves and thorns.

This flock of Merino sheep is grazing in New Zealand. There are 58 million sheep in New Zealand. There are only about 4 million people.

Ship

see also: Barge, Port, Transportation, Waterway

A ship is a vessel that travels over the sea. Some ships carry goods. These are called cargo ships. Giant ships called tankers carry oil. Many countries have ships. They use the ships for protection or in wars.

The first ships

The first known ships were built in Egypt about 6,000 years ago. The first sailing ships were built from wood or bundles of reeds. Ships have had engines for the past 150 years. Ships with engines are faster and more reliable than sailing ships. Today, big ships are built from steel.

People and ships

Ships are the easiest way to send large amounts of goods from one country to another. Almost all long-distance travel used to be by ship. Now much of this traveling is done by airplane.

DID YOU KNOW?

The first settlers who traveled from Europe to the United States and Australia made the journey by ship. Today, most passenger ships are used for vacations. Other ships called ferries travel shorter distances. Ferries carry people and vehicles.

SHIP FIRSTS

FIRST SEA-GOING SHIP	ancient Egypt, 4000 B.C.
FIRST SHIP TO GO AROUND THE WORLD	*The Victoria* in 1522
FIRST STEAM-POWERED SHIP TO CROSS THE ATLANTIC OCEAN	*The Savannah* in 1819

This modern oil tanker is guided into port by smaller boats called tugboats.

The first ships were small. Wooden ships and boats like this one are still used for fishing in India.

Sikhism

Sikhism is a world religion. Its followers are called Sikhs. The word *Sikh* means "learner." The Sikh religion began in northwest India and part of Pakistan. It grew from the teachings of Guru Nanak. He lived nearly 600 years ago.

Beliefs and teachings

Guru Nanak was born in 1469 in the Punjab. He believed that God told him to show people how to follow a simple faith. Nine other gurus followed Guru Nanak. The tenth guru put all the teachings into a book. The book is called the *Guru Granth Sahib*.

Sikhs believe in one God. They believe that God is neither a man nor a woman. They believe that God has no color or rank. Sikhs think about the meaning of God. They try to live their lives with honesty, hard work, and caring.

Sikhism today

There are about 20 million Sikhs all over the world. Most live in India. Sikhs pray at home and in Sikh temples. The temples are called *gurdwaras*. Food is also served in the *gurdwaras*. Festivals called *gurpurbs* mark the anniversaries of the ten Sikh gurus.

Food prepared in the kitchen of the Sikh temple is served at a Sikh wedding.

The book of teachings, Guru Granth Sahib, *is kept on a throne. It is looked after by a special person called a granthi.*

DID YOU KNOW?

Sikhs have five special symbols called *The Five Ks*. The symbols are worn by the Khalsa. They are groups of devout Sikhs.

Singapore

see also: Asia

Singapore is a very small country. It is in southeast Asia. Most of Singapore is on one big island. The weather is always hot and wet. The forests have monkeys and many types of butterflies.

Living in Singapore

Most people work in banks or other office jobs. Many women make parts for computers. Some people have jobs in the docks at the port.

People from China, Malaysia, India, and other countries have come to live in Singapore. Each group has its own festivals. Street parades with dragons and lanterns celebrate the Chinese New Year.

There are many modern buildings in Singapore.

DID YOU KNOW?

The port of Singapore is the largest port in the world.

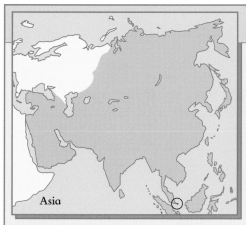

Asia

FACT FILE

PEOPLE	Singaporean
POPULATION	about 4 million
MAIN LANGUAGES	English, Malay, Chinese, Tamil
CAPITAL CITY	Singapore City
MONEY	Singapore dollar
HIGHEST POINT	Bukit Tamah Hill—578 feet

Sitting Bull

Sitting Bull was a Sioux chief, warrior, and spiritual leader. His people lived on the plains of North America.

Sitting Bull becomes chief

Sitting Bull fought in his first battle before he was fourteen. He became the chief of the Hunkpapa. The Hunkpapa was one of several groups that made up the Lakota Sioux tribe. The United States wanted all the Sioux to live on reservations.

Sitting Bull led warriors against U.S. soldiers. By 1868, he was head chief of all the Lakota tribes. In 1876, he led Sioux, Cheyenne, and Arapaho warriors in the Battle of the Little Bighorn.

Sitting Bull talks to General Nelson Miles after the Battle of the Little Bighorn in 1876.

Surrender

The Sioux won the battle, but later they were forced onto reservations. Sitting Bull and hundreds of Hunkpapas escaped to Canada. It was hard to find food. The starving Hunkpapas came back to surrender. They went to live on Standing Rock reservation.

In 1890, U.S. officials became afraid Sitting Bull would tell his people to rise up again. They sent police to get the chief. There was a fight. Sitting Bull was killed.

DID YOU KNOW?

Sitting Bull became a celebrity in 1885. He toured with Buffalo Bill's Wild West show.

This photograph of Sitting Bull was taken in 1881.

Skeleton

see also: Human Body, Vertebrate

A skeleton is the framework of bones that holds up an animal. A skeleton protects the important organs. It helps the animal to move.

The human skeleton

The human body has more than 200 bones joined together to make a skeleton. Living cells make new bones as humans grow. Many of the bones of young babies are not hard. They bend easily. The bones of adults become more brittle. They break more easily.

Joints and moving

The skeleton must have joints to move. Some joints between bones are like the hinges of a door. The bones move but stay fixed together. Ligaments are like strong strings. They hold the bones together at the joints. Tendons are like ligaments. They join the muscles to the bones. Bones are moved when muscles pull on them.

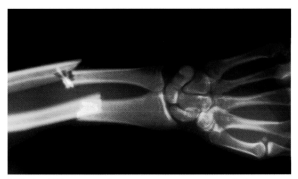

This X-ray shows an arm with two broken bones.

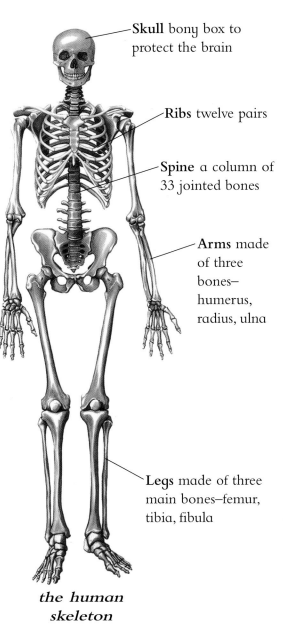

Skull bony box to protect the brain

Ribs twelve pairs

Spine a column of 33 jointed bones

Arms made of three bones— humerus, radius, ulna

Legs made of three main bones—femur, tibia, fibula

the human skeleton

Skunk

see also: Mammal

The skunk is a mammal. It hunts at night. It lives in North America. A skunk is black and white. These colors warn off other animals. A skunk sprays a horrible-smelling liquid on its enemies or when it is frightened.

Skunk families

A skunk often lives in a woodpile. Its home is called a den. Sometimes it shares its den with a fox or a raccoon. Several skunks will share a den in winter. They sleep or rest for several months.

The female skunk gives birth to as many as ten babies. The babies are called kits. She feeds them milk. Kits stay with their mother even after they are old enough to hunt.

glands under the tail spray a bad smelling liquid at enemies

SKUNK FACTS

NUMBER OF KINDS	13
COLOR	black and white
LENGTH	18 inches plus tail
WEIGHT	up to 7 lbs.
STATUS	common
LIFE SPAN	about 7 years
ENEMIES	bobcats, owls, people

fur and fluffy tail to keep warm

sharp claws for digging up food

a skunk

Kits stay close to their den or their mother when they are young.

PLANT, INSECT, AND MEAT EATER

A skunk digs in the soil to find insects. It looks for grasshoppers and beetles. It also digs up worms, roots, and fungi. A skunk will also claw fish out of the water.

Slavery

see also: Civil War; Lincoln, Abraham; Tubman, Harriet

Slavery is the ownership of one person by another. Slaves are bought and sold like animals. They have to do what their owners tell them. They work without being paid.

Many peoples in the distant past had slaves. Often slaves were people from other nations who were captured during wars. The ancient Romans used Greek slaves as teachers.

Slaves in America

In colonial America and later in the United States, many people owned slaves. Early European settlers forced Native Americans to be slaves. Then colonists started to buy African slaves. Slaves from Africa came mostly to the South. Plantation owners used slaves to work in their cotton and tobacco fields.

This village was set up for freed slaves in Virginia during the Civil War.

Slaves worked on cotton plantations in the South.

Being a slave

Slaves brought from Africa were taken from their families. They tried to make new families in America. Sometimes members of their family were sold and taken away. Slaves worked hard. They were often punished. Slaves were not allowed to read or write.

Freedom

Many Americans knew slavery was wrong. Some helped slaves escape to the North. People called abolitionists fought to get rid of slavery. After the Civil War ended, all slaves in the United States were freed.

KEY DATES

1619	First slaves arrive from Africa.
1861	The Civil War begins.
1863	Emancipation Proclamation.
1865	Thirteenth Amendment bans slavery in the United States.

Slovakia

see also: Czech Republic, Europe

Slovakia is a country in central Europe. It has many mountains with forests. The flat land in the south has hot temperatures. Winters are cold. Summers are warm.

Living in Slovakia
Most Slovakians live in the country. Farmers grow grapes, sugar beets, corn, and wheat. Many people work in factories. They make ceramics and machinery.

There are many traditional foods in Slovakia. The spice called paprika is cooked with beef and chicken. Pancakes are filled with chocolate sauce.

Slovakia is famous for making musical instruments. Folk music festivals are held in eastern Slovakia. Local musicians perform at pop music festivals in Bratislava.

St. Martin's Cathedral is one of the tallest buildings in Bratislava.

DID YOU KNOW?

Slovakia and the Czech Republic once formed the country of Czechoslovakia. Slovakia became independent in 1993.

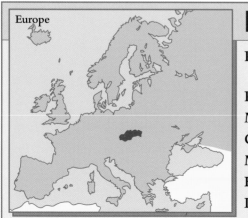

Europe

FACT FILE

PEOPLE	Slovaks, Slovakians
POPULATION	about 5 million
MAIN LANGUAGE	Slovak
CAPITAL CITY	Bratislava
MONEY	Koruna
HIGHEST MOUNTAIN	Gerlachovský Stít—8,710 feet
LONGEST RIVER	Danube River—1,770 miles

Slovenia

see also: Serbia and Montenegro

Slovenia is a country in southeast Europe. There are hills, mountains, and many forests. Summers are warm. Winters are cold. The mountains have heavy snow.

Living in Slovenia

Half the people in Slovenia live in the cities. They work in offices and factories. They mine for coal, lead, zinc, and mercury. Farmers grow cereals, potatoes, and fruit. Some farmers raise sheep, goats, and cattle.

The mountains are popular with tourists. Many people go to the mountains to ski.

A favorite meal in Slovenia is beans and pork. It is cooked with sauerkraut. Sauerkraut is chopped, pickled cabbage. Slovenes enjoy pastries filled with cheese, apples, walnuts, and poppy seeds. The pastries are called *gibanica*.

At some weddings, women wear highly decorated costumes and embroidered hats.

DID YOU KNOW?

Slovene, the language of Slovenia, has 40 different local forms. Different forms of the same language are called dialects.

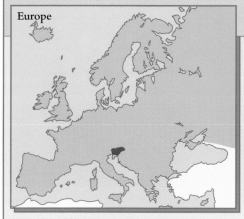

Europe

FACT FILE

PEOPLE	Slovenes, Slovenians
POPULATION	2 million
MAIN LANGUAGE	Slovene
CAPITAL CITY	Ljubljana
MONEY	Tolar
HIGHEST MOUNTAIN	Mount Triglav—9,396 feet
LONGEST RIVER	Sava River—584 miles

Slug

see also: Mollusk, Snail

A slug is a small, slow animal. It has a soft body. Slugs are in the group of animals called mollusks. They have no bones and no legs. Slugs slither on one big foot. Some slugs live on land. Other slugs live in water.

Slug families

Each slug is both a male and a female. Every adult slug can lay eggs.

Slugs move slowly over the ground. They use their feelers to find food. Slugs like damp, cool places because they easily dry out and die.

The slug's big foot leaves a slimy trail on the ground. This helps the rest of its body to slip along.

SLUG FACTS

NUMBER OF KINDS	more than 35 thousand kinds of slugs and snails
COLOR	black, brown, or brightly colored
SIZE	up to 4 inches long
STATUS	common
LIFE SPAN	up to 7 years
ENEMIES	mammals such as hedgehogs and shrews

feelers to taste and smell the air

soft, slimy body

a gray garden slug

PLANT EATER

Slugs come out to feed mostly at night. They eat shoots, lichen, fungi, and algae. Slugs can't chew. A slug has a special rough tongue. It is rough like a nail file. This grates up the food into little pieces.

Slug eggs are laid near food so the babies have plenty to eat.

Smell

see also: Taste, Touch

Smell is one of the five senses. It helps animals and people find out about things around them. Human beings and some other animals use their noses to smell things.

How smelling works

Nearly everything has a smell. The nose takes in air. The cells in the nose send signals to the brain. People and animals get to know the smell of different objects.

Using smells

Smells can warn people of danger. People smell smoke when there is a fire. They smell gas if there is a gas leak. People smell food to find out if the food is good to eat. Animals use their sense of smell to help them find food. Animals also use smells to find a mate and to know if enemies are near. Some animals leave a scent to mark their territory or to find their way back home.

Air is taken in through the nose.

The air passes cells called smell receptors. The receptors send messages about the smell to the brain.

Air that is taken in through the mouth does not pass the smell receptors. The brain does not get a message about the smell.

the human nose and how smelling works

Snail

see also: Mollusk, Slug

A snail is a small, slow animal. It has a soft body. Snails belong to the group of animals called mollusks. Snails have no legs. They slither along on one big foot. They carry their shells on their backs. Snails live all over the world. They live in water and on land.

SNAIL FACTS

NUMBER OF KINDS	more than 35 thousand kinds of slugs and snails
COLOR	many colors
LENGTH	up to 24 inches
WEIGHT	up to 32 ounces
STATUS	common
LIFE SPAN	up to 7 years
ENEMIES	birds, people

Snail families

Each snail is a male and a female. Every snail can lay eggs. Snails lay eggs near plenty of food for the baby snails to eat when they hatch.

a shell is a snail's home

a garden snail

eyes on stalks

feelers to taste and smell the air

one big foot to slither on

These garden snail eggs are just hatching.

PLANT AND MEAT EATER

Snails eat plants and other snails. They can't chew. A snail has a special rough tongue. It is rough like a nail file. This grates up the food into little pieces.

Snake

see also: Reptile

A snake is a reptile. It has no legs and a long, thin body. Snakes live almost all over the world. They do not live in the very coldest places. Some snakes that live in cold places hibernate in the winter. Many snakes live on land. Some can live in water.

SNAKE FACTS

NUMBER OF KINDS	2,000
COLOR	many colors and patterns
LENGTH	up to 33 feet
WEIGHT	up to 550 lbs.
STATUS	cobras are rare
LIFE SPAN	up to 30 years
ENEMIES	other snakes, people

a Gaboon viper snake

scales keep the body from drying out

pointed head to push through soft ground and thick plants

jaws that unhinge and open extra wide to swallow big animals

Snake families

Most female snakes lay as many as ten eggs. They cover the eggs or bury them in the ground. The eggs hatch into baby snakes. Some snake babies are born alive. These snakes do not hatch from eggs. Baby snakes look after themselves as soon as they hatch or are born.

MEAT EATER

All snakes are hunters. They eat meat. Snakes eat mammals, birds, and other reptiles. Snakes swallow their prey whole. The swallowed food looks like a big lump as it squeezes down through the snake's body.

Snakes have many ways of killing their food. Rattlesnakes have a poisonous bite. Boa constrictors crush their victims. This python has opened its jaw wide to swallow a whole gazelle.

Soil

see also: Crop, Farming

Soil is made up of small, broken bits of rock, minerals, plants, and animals. Soil covers most of the solid ground in the world. It takes thousands of years for bigger pieces of rock, minerals, and rotted plants and animals to become soil.

Different kinds of soil

Humus is soil with lots of bits of dead plants and animals in it. Humus in soil helps the soil hold water. Many plants grow well in humus. Farmers and gardeners say that the soil is fertile when plants are growing well.

Clay is soil with very, very small particles. Clay is very sticky. It can be used to make bricks or pottery.

Sandy soils are made from larger particles. They are easy to dig. Humus or special chemicals called fertilizers must be added to sandy soils to keep them fertile.

This big gulley was made by erosion. Erosion happens when plants are cut down and there are no roots to hold soil together. Soil is then blown or washed away.

Cutting down trees and hedges makes huge fields for growing crops.

DID YOU KNOW?

Worms help make soil better for plants. Worms make spaces in the soil for the air to get in. They pull parts of dead plants and animals down into the soil.

Solar System

see also: Space Exploration, Spacecraft

A solar system is all of the objects that orbit a star. The objects include planets, moons, and asteroids. The solar system that includes Earth is made up of the sun, nine planets and their moons, millions of asteroids, and some comets.

NICOLAUS COPERNICUS (1473–1543)

People once believed that everything in the sky moved around the earth. Then the Polish astronomer Copernicus wrote about what he saw in the sky. Copernicus showed that the earth and other planets moved around the sun.

Solar systems and gravity

Solar systems are held together by gravity. All objects have gravity forces. This force pulls other things toward an object. The gravity of larger objects is stronger than the force of smaller objects. The sun's gravity pulls on all the planets. It keeps the planets in their orbits.

Our solar system probably began as a big cloud of gas and dust. Most of the gas formed the sun. The leftover gas and dust made the planets and comets.

The planets in our solar system that are near to the sun are rocky and quite small. These are Mercury, Venus, Earth, and Mars. The planets further away are much bigger and not solid. These are Jupiter, Saturn, Uranus, and Neptune. Pluto is small even though it is the farthest from the sun. The sun's gravity probably pulled Pluto into orbit after the other planets were in place. There is a ring of smaller, rocky lumps called asteroids between Mars and Jupiter.

All the planets in our solar system and the asteroid belt orbit the sun. This model also shows a comet.

Somalia

see also: Africa

Somalia is a country in east Africa. It is flat and sandy along the coast. There are hills in the north. A small amount of rain falls between March and May. Somalia is mostly very dry, except in the south.

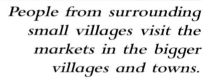

People from surrounding small villages visit the markets in the bigger villages and towns.

Living in Somalia

Most people in Somalia are nomads. They do not stay in one place. Nomads move to find food and water for their herds. They keep goats, sheep, cattle, and camels. Their homes are made from skins or mats stretched over wooden frames.

Many Somalis eat *anan geil*. This is millet cooked with camel's milk and honey. Poetry, folk tales, and history are very important to Somalis. *Dab-Shid* is the Somali New Year festival of fire and light. It is celebrated with feasts and big bonfires.

DID YOU KNOW?

The ancient perfumes called frankincense and myrrh are collected as sap from trees in Somalia.

FACT FILE

PEOPLE	Somalis
POPULATION	about 8 million
MAIN LANGUAGES	Somali, Arabic
CAPITAL CITY	Mogadishu
MONEY	Somali shilling
HIGHEST MOUNTAIN	Mount Surad—7,903 feet
LONGEST RIVER	Webi Shaballe—1,199 miles

Africa

Sound

see also: Ear

Sounds are the noises that people and animals hear. Sounds are caused by vibrations. These are tiny forward and backward movements. Sound waves are made by the vibrations. The vibrations are picked up by the ears of humans and animals. Sound travels in invisible waves. It goes through air, liquids, and solids.

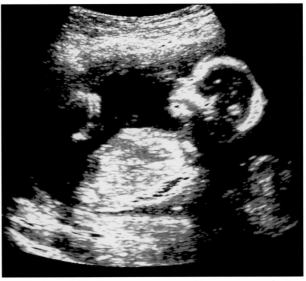

This ultrasound picture was made from echoes bouncing off a baby that is inside its mother.

Kinds of sound

Different vibrations make different sounds. Most sounds are a mixture of vibrations. Vibrations are big in loud sounds. High sounds made by a whistle have very quick vibrations. Low sounds like thunder have slow vibrations.

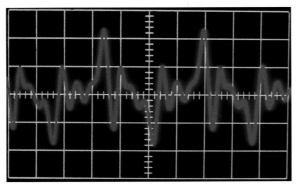

The red line shows the sound waves of a note played by a harmonica. Everything from a human voice to a musical instrument has its own special pattern of vibrations.

Speed of sound

Sound travels more than 958 feet in a second. This is a speed of about 745 miles per hour. Some airplanes travel faster than sound. They can go faster than the sound they make. If sound hits something hard, such as a wall or a cliff, it bounces off. Sound that travels back to where it was made is called an echo.

DID YOU KNOW?

Some sounds are so high-pitched that the human ear cannot hear them. This type of sound is called ultrasonic or ultrasound. Doctors use ultrasound to make echoes inside the human body. Then special machines use the echoes to make pictures of what is inside the body.

South Africa

see also: Africa

South Africa is a country in Africa. Most of the land is high and flat. The northwest has hot, dry deserts. The south has mountains. It rains from October to April.

Living in South Africa

About half of the people live in cities. Farmers in rural areas raise animals. They grow grain and fruit. Mining is very important in South Africa.

People from other countries have moved to South Africa over the past 300 years. This makes the South African people a mix of black Africans, Dutch, British, and Asians. The customs, food, and religions of all of these people are part of South Africa today.

Townships like this one grew up around all of the big towns and cities in South Africa. This happened during the time when black South Africans were not allowed to live in the cities.

DID YOU KNOW?

Nelson Mandela was elected as the country's first black president in 1994. He fought for the rights of black South Africans. Mandela spent 27 years in prison for his beliefs.

Africa

FACT FILE

PEOPLE	South Africans
POPULATION	almost 43 million
MAIN LANGUAGES	Afrikaans, English, African languages
CAPITAL CITY	Pretoria, Cape Town, Bloemfontein
BIGGEST CITY	Cape Town
MONEY	Rand
HIGHEST MOUNTAIN	Thaban-Ntlenyana—11,428 feet
LONGEST RIVER	Orange River—1,300 miles

South America

see also: Continent

South America is the fourth largest continent. The Atlantic Ocean is along the east coast. The Pacific Ocean is along the west coast.

The land

The Andes Mountains stretch the whole length of South America. They are along the western side. Some of the highest mountains are active volcanoes. The Amazon River and many smaller rivers flow across the flat land in the north.

Climate, plants, and animals

It is always hot and wet in the Amazon area. Most of the land around the Amazon River is covered by rain forest. Animals such as hummingbirds, armadillos, and monkeys live in the rain forest. Grasslands in the south are called the *pampas*.

People in South America

There are about 349 million people in South America. Some are Native American people. Others are related to people who came from Spain and Portugal. There are also descendants of slaves from Africa. This mix of people live together in twelve different countries.

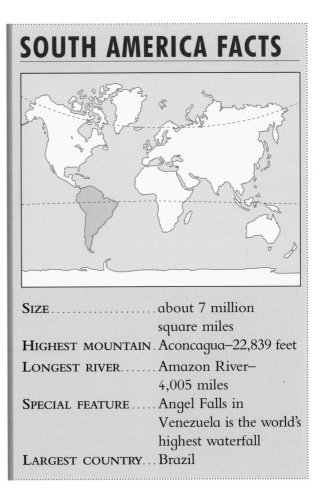

SOUTH AMERICA FACTS

SIZE	about 7 million square miles
HIGHEST MOUNTAIN	Aconcagua–22,839 feet
LONGEST RIVER	Amazon River–4,005 miles
SPECIAL FEATURE	Angel Falls in Venezuela is the world's highest waterfall
LARGEST COUNTRY	Brazil

This huge bird is the Andean Condor. It can be seen flying high over many countries in South America. It has a wingspan of nearly ten feet.

South Carolina

see also: United States of America

South Carolina is a state in the southeastern United States of America. There are forested hills in the northwest of the state. The center and coastal regions are lowlands. The weather is hot and humid.

In the past

Charleston was an important city in the South. Its harbor was used for shipping cotton and tobacco. Charleston's forts were attacked in the American Revolution and in the Civil War. Today, Charleston is still a busy port.

This is a photograph of Boone Hall Plantation in South Carolina.

> ## DID YOU KNOW?
>
> African Americans in South Carolina have tried to keep their ancestors' traditions alive. People in the Sea Islands along the coast speak Gullah, a mix of English and African languages.

Life in South Carolina

South Carolina has many factories producing clothes and other textile products. Farms in the state raise tobacco, cotton, and chickens. Fishermen and women catch shrimp and other seafood along the coast. Many tourists come to the state to visit its beaches, gardens, and historic sites.

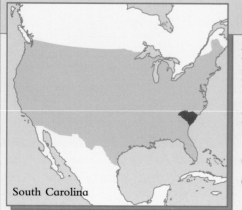

South Carolina

FACT FILE

BECAME A STATE	1788 (8th state)
LAND AREA	30,109 square miles (40th largest land area)
POPULATION	4,147,152 (25th most populated state)
OTHER NAME	Palmetto State
CAPITAL CITY	Columbia

South Dakota

see also: United States of America

South Dakota is a state in the northern United States of America. Most of the state is on the Great Plains. In the east are hills and grassland. The Black Hills are mountains in the west of the state. In South Dakota, summers are very hot and winters are very cold.

Bison still roam at Custer State Park, South Dakota.

In the past

The Black Hills are a sacred place to the Sioux people of South Dakota. In the 1800s, they were part of the Great Sioux Reservation. In 1874, the U.S. Army found gold in the Black Hills. Soon, gold miners came and built towns there. The Sioux had to give up their land.

Mount Rushmore is in the Black Hills. Giant faces of four U.S. presidents are carved into the mountain. Many visitors come to see Mount Rushmore.

DID YOU KNOW?

The Badlands are rocky hills in southwestern South Dakota. The hills have been carved into strange shapes by wind and water.

Life in South Dakota

Much of South Dakota is grazing land for cattle. Farmers also produce corn, sunflower seeds, flaxseed, hay, and rye. Many factories in the state process the food raised there. They also make machinery and electronic equipment.

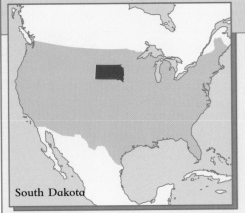

South Dakota

FACT FILE

BECAME A STATE...	1889 (40th state)
LAND AREA.........	75,885 square miles (16th largest land area)
POPULATION	764,309 (46th most populated state)
OTHER NAMES	Mount Rushmore State, Coyote State
CAPITAL CITY	Pierre

South Korea

see also: Asia, North Korea

South Korea is a country on the east coast of Asia. Most of South Korea is covered by hills and mountains. There are thousands of small islands off the west coast. The weather is cold and dry in the winter. It is hot and very wet in the summer.

> ## DID YOU KNOW?
> The 1988 summer Olympic Games were held in the capital city of Seoul.

Living in South Korea
Most South Koreans work in offices and in factories. South Koreans makes ships, cars, and electrical goods. These goods are sold all over the world. Farmers grow rice and vegetables. Mulberries are grown to feed to silkworms.

The people in South Korea are very proud of their past. There are many traditional Korean customs, special music, and dances. The martial arts sport of *tae kwon do* comes from South Korea.

The people in this small town live in small houses with different colored roofs.

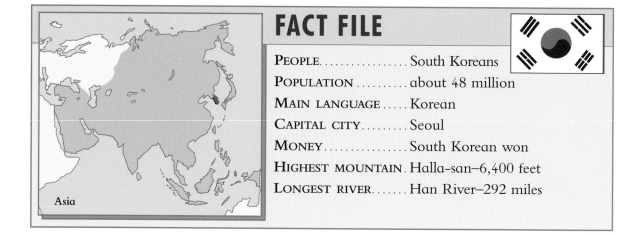

Asia

FACT FILE

PEOPLE	South Koreans
POPULATION	about 48 million
MAIN LANGUAGE	Korean
CAPITAL CITY	Seoul
MONEY	South Korean won
HIGHEST MOUNTAIN	Halla-san—6,400 feet
LONGEST RIVER	Han River—292 miles

Space Exploration

see also: Moon, Planet, Spacecraft

People have looked out into space since ancient times. People have been traveling into space for only a short time. Today most space exploration uses telescopes or robot probes.

The first space exploration

The first satellite, *Sputnik 1,* was sent into space by the Russians in 1957. Twelve years later, the American *Apollo 11* mission put men on the moon. Space probes have now been to all of the planets except Pluto. Other probes have flown close to comets.

This is an artist's drawing of Sputnik 1. It was the first man-made satellite to orbit the earth. It was made of aluminum and had four hanging antennas.

Telescopes

Telescopes are used to see objects millions of miles away in space. The first telescope was invented in 1608. People have been exploring space with telescopes ever since that time. All the known comets have been discovered by people looking through telescopes. Today, telescopes are getting bigger and more powerful.

This robot was used in 1997 in the unmanned exploration of Mars.

DID YOU KNOW?

An astrophysicist is someone who studies what makes up the things in space.

Spacecraft

see also: Moon, Space Exploration

A spacecraft is a machine that travels into space. Unmanned spacecraft have no people inside. Manned spacecraft carry people inside them. People that go into space are called astronauts.

The first spacecraft

The first spacecraft to carry a person into space was launched in 1961. It was fixed to a large rocket and fired into space. Most spacecraft do not carry people. They take computers and other scientific equipment into space. They send pictures and information about space back to Earth.

SPACECRAFT FIRSTS

FIRST SPACECRAFT	*Sputnik 1*, 1957 Soviet Union (Russia)
FIRST PERSON IN SPACE	Yuri Gagarin, Soviet Union April 1961
FIRST AMERICAN IN SPACE	Alan Shepard, Jr., May 1961
FIRST MANNED MOONLANDING	*Apollo 11* mission, 1969
FIRST TRIP BY SPACE SHUTTLE	April 12, 1981

How we use spacecraft

Spacecraft can take pictures of far away planets. Spacecraft such as satellites can be used for bouncing TV pictures and telephone calls around the world.

The United States space shuttle is attached to a large launch rocket.

American astronauts on the moon traveled in an electric vehicle. It was called a lunar rover.

Spain

see also: Europe

Spain is a country in southwest Europe. The center of Spain has a high, flat area. It is crossed by mountain ranges. Summers are hot and dry. Winters can be cold with some snow.

Living in Spain

Many people in Spain live in the cities. They work in offices, factories, and in the tourist trade. Farmers grow crops such as wheat, oranges, and olives. They also raise animals.

A popular Spanish meal is *paella*. This is rice cooked with a spice called saffron. The saffron colors the rice yellow. The rice is mixed with meat and fish.

Flamenco dance has been performed in southern Spain for hundreds of years. The dancers wear special, colorful costumes. Flamenco is a mix of gypsy and North African dance.

This cathedral in Barcelona was started in 1883. It is still not finished because the architect died without leaving any plans.

DID YOU KNOW?

The famous modern artist, Pablo Picasso (1881–1973), was born in Spain. Many people say that Picasso was the most important artist of the 20th century.

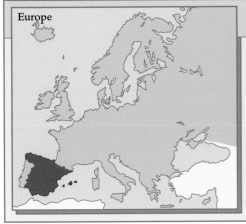

Europe

FACT FILE

PEOPLE	Spanish, Spaniards
POPULATION	about 40 million
MAIN LANGUAGES	Spanish, Catalan, Galician, Basque
CAPITAL CITY	Madrid
MONEY	Euro
HIGHEST MOUNTAIN	Mulhacén—11,415 feet
LONGEST RIVER	Guadiana—515 miles

Spider

see also: Invertebrate

A spider is a small animal with eight legs. Many spiders spin webs to catch food. Spiders have been on the earth since the time of the dinosaurs.

Spider families

Female spiders lay eggs that hatch into baby spiders. Spider babies are called spiderlings. Spiderlings cannot hunt or spin webs until they are full size.

Spiders trap animals in their webs. Then they bite the trapped animals. Spiders have pointed fangs that are like teeth. Their sharp fangs pump their prey full of poison.

tubes to make silk for spinning webs

hairs on the body and legs help spiders see and hear

some spiderlings travel on their mother's back

weak eyes that are not very useful

a wolf spider

Spiders use their strong webs to trap and store food.

INSECT AND MEAT EATER

Spiders mainly eat insects. Without spiders, there would be too many insects in the world. Some very big spiders can eat small birds. Some spiders have bites that are poisonous enough to kill people.